MAGNETS

Troll Associates

MAGNETS

by Laurence Santrey

Illustrated by Joseph Veno

Troll Associates

Library of Congress Cataloging in Publication Data

Santrey, Laurence.
  Magnets.

  Summary: Discusses the qualities of magnets, which
attract certain metals and have been used as compasses
and as components of many modern inventions, including
the telephone, television, and electric motor.
    1. Magnets—Juvenile literature.   [1. Magnets.
2. Magnetism]   I. Veno, Joseph, ill.   II. Title.
QC757.5.S26   1984   538'.2   84-2597
ISBN 0-8167-0140-7 (lib. bdg.)
ISBN 0-8167-0141-5 (pbk.)

10 9 8 7 6 5 4 3 2 1

The magnet is one of nature's greatest mysteries. It has a wonderful kind of power. Almost magically, a magnet can pull things to itself. It can make a nail jump to it and stick there. A magnet can draw one paper clip to itself, then another, and another—and they all stick together in a long chain, as if they were glued.

When these things happen, we say that the magnet is attracting. But a magnet doesn't attract everything. You can't use a magnet to pick up a glass or a rubber ball or a handkerchief. That's because these objects are not made of the metals that are attracted to magnets. Only things with the metals iron, nickel, or cobalt in them are attracted to magnets.

If you put a magnet next to a spoon and they come together, you know the spoon has either iron, nickel, or cobalt in it. You can try the same test with anything else made of metal. If it has iron, nickel, or cobalt in it, it will be attracted to the magnet.

10

You are probably familiar with two kinds of magnets—bar magnets and horseshoe magnets. A bar magnet is straight and flat. Sometimes bar magnets are used to hold doors shut. Your refrigerator door probably has bar magnets around its edges to keep it tightly closed.

A horseshoe magnet is a bar magnet that has been bent into the shape of a horseshoe. These magnets are sometimes used as toys, but they are also an important part of most small electric motors.

Other kinds of magnets are made in the shape of cylinders or disks. These magnets are used in different kinds of machines and in telephones, televisions, radios, and loud-speaker systems.

Hundreds of years went by before anyone put magnetite to real use. Then sailors found a way to make a compass with the strange stones. They took a long, thin piece of magnetite and put it on a piece of wood. Then they floated the wood in a bowl of water. The same end of the magnetite always pointed in the same direction—north.

With this simple compass, sailors did not have to depend on the sun or the stars to guide them. Because the magnetic stone gave them their direction, it came to be called a *lodestone*. The word *lode* means "to lead." The lodestone was a stone that would always lead the way.

Every magnet, no matter how big or small it is, has a north pole and a south pole. The north pole of a magnet will always attract the south pole of another magnet. So we say that opposite poles attract.

But if one pole of a magnet is brought near the same pole of another magnet, the two poles will push away from each other. We say that like poles, or similar poles, repel.

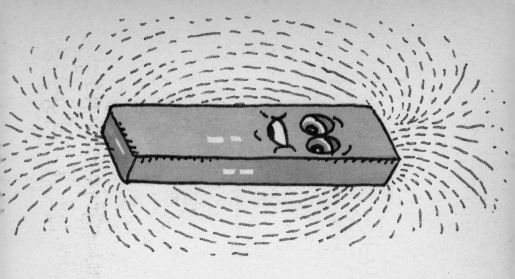

Around every magnet there's a special area where its attraction or "pulling power" works. This area is called a magnetic field. The magnet's field reaches out in lines called lines of force.

Scientists have a way to show how these lines of force act. They put a piece of paper on top of a magnet. Then they sprinkle tiny bits of iron, called iron filings, over the paper. Next, they tap the paper gently, and the iron filings move into a fan-shaped pattern around the two ends of the magnet.

This pattern is caused by the lines of force at each end of the magnet. It gives a clear picture of the magnetic field around the magnet.

A magnet's magnetic field is strongest at its north and south poles. The field is weakest in the center of the magnet. The same thing is true of Earth's magnetic field. It is strongest near the north and south magnetic poles.

For that reason, a compass works better when it is closer to one of these poles. At the equator, which is an imaginary line running around Earth's center, a compass does not work very well. That's because the equator is at the center of Earth's magnetic field.

Just as Earth is a magnet, everything on Earth and in our entire universe has magnetism. Stars and planets in faraway galaxies have magnetic fields. So do the tiny atoms and molecules that make up everything in the universe. Then why doesn't everything stick together, like iron filings to a magnet?

Scientists explain it this way. In just about everything, molecules point in all directions. Their magnetic fields are not lined up in a regular order. So they do not have much force.

But in a magnet, all the molecules are lined up in the *same* direction. All the north poles of the molecules point in one direction, and all the south poles point in the opposite direction. Together they set up a powerful magnetic field.

You can make a magnet weaker by upsetting its magnetic field. To do this, heat or bang a magnet very hard. This makes the molecules jump out of line. When the molecules jump around, they pull in many different directions. And this weakens the magnetic field.

Breaking a magnet itself into two or more small parts doesn't weaken it at all. It just makes two or more magnets that are smaller.

This fact was discovered by a French engineer in the year 1269. He broke a piece off the north-pole end of a magnet and a piece off the south-pole end. He wanted to see if the piece from the north-pole end would have only north-pole qualities, and if the piece from the south-pole end would have only south-pole qualities. But what he found was that *every* piece of the original magnet was a full magnet with its own north and south poles.

A scientist from Denmark, named Hans Christian Oersted, made another important discovery about magnetism. He learned that magnetism can be produced by electricity. How did he do this?

First, Oersted connected a wire to an electric battery. Then he put the wire next to a compass. When the battery was turned on, its current made the compass needle swing away from its north-south position and point at the live wire. When the current was turned off, the compass needle swung back to its north-south position.

This experiment proved that an electric current sets up a magnetic field that attracts a compass needle. It also proves that electricity produces magnetism.

An English scientist, named Michael Faraday, made another important discovery. He showed that, just as electricity produces magnetism, magnets can be used to produce electricity.

The scientific work done by Oersted and Faraday led to many of today's inventions. One of these is the electromagnet. A huge electromagnet can be used to pick up very large, heavy pieces of metal, such as cars and trucks.

Electromagnets are also used in a machine called a synchrotron. A synchrotron is a modern instrument used by scientists in atom-smashing experiments.

Another important invention is the giant electric generator known as a dynamo. A dynamo uses huge electromagnets to produce large amounts of electricity. This electricity is then fed into our homes, schools, office buildings, and factories.

An electromagnet can be very powerful. But it is only a *temporary* magnet. That means that its magnetism does not last. When the electrical current is turned off, the magnetism disappears. Other magnets are *permanent*. That means that their magnetism *does* last. The lodestone is a natural magnet and has permanent magnetism.

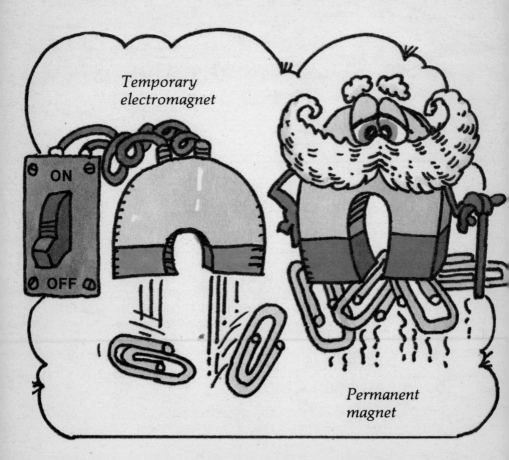

Temporary electromagnet

ON

OFF

Permanent magnet

You can make a magnet yourself. All you need is an iron nail and a magnet. Stroke the magnet against the nail, over and over, about twenty times. Always stroke in the same direction. That way you bring the molecules of the nail into line, the way they are in the magnet itself. You can now use the nail as a magnet. It will lift other nails or paper clips. And if you want to demagnetize the nail, or make it lose its magnetism, just rap it against a hard surface a few times.

All magnets have one thing in common, whether they are magnets you make yourself or the magnets in a small compass or the largest electromagnets. They all have the magical power to attract certain metals and to create a force field that makes things work.

Without magnets and magnetism, we wouldn't have telephones or radios. We wouldn't have television sets or electric motors or thousands of other scientific wonders we use every day. The world would be a much different place without nature's marvelous gift—magnetism!